“Go Dark.”

Inspiration, Growth, Results

By Alexander Bejar

Contents

Preface

Most people do not write books at my age. In fact, most people these days don't really "read" books. The thing being that in an age of technology, we would rather watch a summary or video on the topic rather than actually read the original work but in that retrospect, I am only speculating, not speaking on behalf of my generation. Maybe one day I will look back on this and say, "Why on earth did I write this?" but maybe it will serve purpose to you.

This book is a collection of quotes that I, myself, have come up with or, with quotations cited, are statements I tend to find true and relative to any situation throughout life. The power of philosophy is not in its metaphorical dogma or it's elegance; it is within the interpretation of it by the writer, the speaker, but most importantly, the receiver of its intended effect, whether it be heard among the masses, written within the archives, or even kept intact by historians after my time has passed.

Remember the importance of educating yourself, but also remember as much as it is beneficial to dabble within philosophy, be cautious of the deception of becoming wise in your own eyes. The many individuals I have met that have become high and mighty through their own version of perfection have always fallen and crumbled into dust. The purpose of philosophy is not to judge others, or to criticize the many religious factions of the world, or even to prove you are "woke". It is to apply the very same laws and life lessons we all experience, regardless of affiliation, belief, or cause, to our everyday lives and the interpretation of their meanings.

We have a word for this. We call it **Opinion**.

I thank you for reading the wisdom I have accumulated over the last 3 years. It has been a long journey, but it has been the most dynamic, enlightening 3 years of my life and to think, it took a trip to White Sands, New Mexico to change my perspective

...But that is a story for another time.

-Alexander Bejar

Dedicated to my family, Jose & Romie Bejar, and Trevor & Kayla Gregg. Thank you for supporting my efforts always.

Honorable mentions:

The Trading Fraternity, also called "Chad", or "The Cult".

Chapter 1: Validity

"Seeking Validation from others only invalidates yourself."

The first ever proverb written by myself came from my observation of others fiercely competing in the world during the global Coronavirus pandemic. Our vulnerability was exposed during the onslaught of what we would call the most turbulent section of modern history post millennium. As I contemplated the events unfolding in the time of my early 20's, my desire to right myself from the path I had been led on was strengthened.

Today, we have become dependent on the validation of many sources such as social media, our colleagues, our parents, and our friend groups. Many compare themselves to others, wishing to outperform or at least match their achievements in the hopes of being recognized, despite the fact that our unique life is just as special and important. I'm not saying that it is wrong to improve yourself or surpass goals alongside others. What I'm saying is the purpose of these things is to become a better person through self-fulfillment and not through trying to outperform others. It has become a snare and sense of burden rather than an inspiration.

This road we call life has many different paths in it. The journey may be long or short, and the many individuals we come across can teach us many different lessons, despite our differences. These differences are what make us human, and in retrospect stem from our desire to be unique among the many humans we share this planet with. Our seeking for other's approval has made us dependent on what society deems popular or wise, what is to be praised or what is to be shamed. Validation is the concept of justifying our decisions or accolades. It is not a bad thing, but the moment it becomes all we can think of in order to prove our self-worth, it is no better than trying to be what we are not.

It is important to remember that your own success and happiness are not dependent on the validation or approval of others. Your worth and value as a person should not be based on external factors, but rather on your own personal qualities and characteristics. It is essential to focus on your own goals and aspirations, rather than trying to please others. It can be easy to get caught up in seeking validation from others, but it is important to remember that true success and happiness come from your dedication to yourself. Focusing on your own success and personal growth is a far more fulfilling and rewarding pursuit than attempting to please everyone else because at the end of the day, they are not in your mind while you lay in bed, asking yourself if you really are living your own life. It is important to trust in yourself and your own abilities, and to have confidence in your own path and journey towards success.

Therefore, be not so hasty in trying to please others. Fulfill all your endeavors to the best of your ability, and your validation will come from your satisfaction from your work. Enjoying our lives is similar to a meal. We must enjoy it and savor it because it does not last as long as we want, it lasts as long as we make it.

"*Our opportunities outlast our setbacks*."

Chapter 2: Standards

"Do not lower your standards for others. Let them try to follow yours."

You will notice my usage of the word "try". There is a reason for that word in this proverb. Trying is the utilization of your willpower to accomplish something that may be deemed a prerequisite or even a challenge to fulfill an objective.

The usage of the word try implies that not everyone will think or even acknowledge your requirements in different parts of everyday life. These can be as simple as your preferred foods or as complicated as your investment portfolio. The possibilities are endless in the realm of standards. The most common are the qualities looked for in a partner; the search for true love has been at the forefront of a majority of stories for centuries and continues to be the best-selling type of story that Hollywood can sell.

There is nothing wrong with having standards. Many places and peoples do. It is normal human nature to have your preference prioritized over others, especially if you don't know them. Maintaining your standards means setting clear expectations for yourself and holding yourself accountable to them. It is important to have standards for yourself in order to live a fulfilling and meaningful life. Standards can help you to stay focused and motivated, and to make progress towards your goals. That does not mean to be arrogant or selfish in society. The standards people set for themselves are their own choice, but there comes a time when an individual may become unrealistic in their own desires.

Do not be deceived by what the world should look like to you. Be inspired that there is many varieties of life to be had and experienced, regardless of the effect it may have on you. There is much to learn from the world itself. Who knows, you may even find what you weren't looking for.

The proverb's interpretation is not to discourage you from leading by example or to become "soft". It is to encourage you that your own path may not be followed by everyone, but that does not mean the path itself cannot be restructured. People can change, and in change, we may discover there is more to offer from our opened eyes rather our narrow views.

It is essential to be consistent in upholding your standards and not allowing yourself to compromise or settle for less than you deserve. It is important to remember that your standards should be based on your own values and beliefs, not those of others. Maintaining your standards may mean making difficult decisions or standing up for what you believe in, but it is important to stay true to yourself. It is important to review and evaluate your standards regularly to ensure that they are still aligned with your goals and values. Ultimately, maintaining your standards is about living a life that is authentic and true to yourself. It is about being proud of who you are and what you stand for.

"Our standards do not define us; they only help to align our paths with those we were destined to meet."

Chapter 3: The light in the dark

"The littlest of lights shines the brightest in the darkest of nights."

Light. The one thing that lets us know that the day of the worker is upon us. The light shines brightly throughout the world, and its rays shimmer down from the star we call the sun. The light is what lets nature know that a new day has begun and the time to wake and go about the day is here. It is what we enjoy throughout our lives. Light is the one thing we can all associate with being alive and awake, and the joy that comes from being in it.

Close your eyes and imagine a field of green, stretching forth among the land, with large mountains and white fluffy clouds stretching across the bright blue sky! Smell the fresh air and scents of flowers, while your ears are filled with the calls of birds flying over the refreshing sound of a bubbly stream.

This is the canvas of light across the world. It reveals many things, good or evil. The light is what we associate with good and guidance over our travels throughout the world. It is responsible for revealing things that may not be seen in the cover of night or even showing us different perspectives across the roads we travel.

Now stop imagining that. Keep your eyes closed. What do you see?

Darkness. The absence of light.

The lesson in this proverb is the darkness may envelop us. It frightens us at times, especially if we don't know where we are. One lost in the woods may become disoriented and frantic if they cannot see what is around them and if they should encounter danger, not know where to reach safety. The first thing many do when they are in the dark is to search for a source of light. It is to help them see where they are and how to get out. It is not a sign of weakness or fear at times. It is simply common sense. One requires light to do things, lest they make a mistake or get hurt.

However, like many times in life, we may be surrounded by darkness. Our hope acts as light most of the time, or the hope of others to some. We can become lost on our journey through life but sometimes, it takes only one glimmer of hope to help us return to the path we were once on originally and safely. That same glimmer of hope can come from the kind stranger, lending out their hand to help us back on track and sharing their light with yours.

Darkness is not a thing to be afraid of. It is to be respected, and we all travel through the dark at times, but it does no harm, when you have light with you and the darker the night, the brighter the light.

"*Have hope, and hope will have you.*"

Chapter 4: Paths

"The divergence of one's path is not it's end friend. It is the start of a new beginning."

I had a young friend who passed at the age of 17 due to cancer by the name of Logan Earhart. He had just celebrated his birthday despite his condition which had worsened. Logan was an individual who spoke it like it was. He did not easily take things at face value, and his wit made him a very spontaneous and well-liked person. I remember those days like it was yesterday, which now have become a memory in which I have secured to my remembrance forever. Logan had been in remission of brain cancer, but it came back for another fight. Logan fought on for a lengthy time, giving the biggest fight he could muster but eventually, left the path of my life to take another in the afterlife. We all wanted him to stay, but it was time for his journey to begin a new direction. Logan was an inspiration to me, because despite his condition, he went out with a smile on his face and a fist to cancers while he stepped across life into death. His fight was finally over.

All set forth on a path at birth, regardless of how they brought into the world. Some have the luxury of wealth and a life of leisure. Some have poverty and war amongst the people. The majority often are brought in with the bare necessities and must work for the finer in life. They are usually not lacking, but they do not have abundance of many things. The rich, the poor, and the working individual all have one thing in common: They set forth on the path of life.

Some of these individuals climb the ranks through work, whether it be by sheer luck or diligence in their area of expertise. Some of them fall from grace, crashing into the ground, never to rise again. Their accolades, riches and honor a mere memory in the farthest reaches of any hopeful thought. Some never move from their positions, toiling away at life until their very last breath. This is the path of life and there are many different one's to take along it.

The path of one's journey may be abruptly cut short, through death, or it may take a detour through a dark time in order to strengthen them for a new mission in life. The paths we take are not always ones we intend on taking. It is our choice to pursue them as they come along and whether our judgement is sound. This is called decision making. The consequences of our actions can be diverse at times, favoring good or evil, temptation or opportunity, life or death. The choice lies within you.

We learn quickly in life that things happen for no reason at all or with all the reason one could reason with. Our paths intertwine, they diverge, and sometimes they take us to extremes we have never gone to before such as the beauty of the highest mountaintops and the lowest of the most desolate of valley's.

But all in all, one thing remains true:

"The path taken by the few may make all the difference."

Chapter 5: Remembrance

"Remember those who have supported you along the way. Spend time with them."

There are those who we meet along our journey's, through a moment, a life changing event, or by mutual interests. A lot of times, these individuals guide us, befriend us, and mentor us, offering wealth of wisdom of the things they have experienced or of those they have encountered along their own journey's. We can learn a lot from these people. They are called family, lovers, business partners, teachers, and philosophers of old. Our support we receive from those who believe in our goals or share them, is to be cherished. There may come a day that you will have to depart from each other, onto different pathways.

It is not a terrible thing. Change is good, but remember the moments spent with those that have gone on to better and greater things. It is not always death that divides us from our life's journey; it can be a job, marriage, school, children, or just life. We have all lost at one point yet have in return gained, despite the circumstances. Experience comes with age, and age comes with experience, guiding us to record these moments and to learn from them, and the others in their own recollection.

Smile, laugh, cry, console, love, grieve, live through the moments shared together and the lessons they teach us. The most important thing about memories is the people you shared them with and how they impacted you for your personal growth. Do not forget them and be thankful for the opportunity to grow as an individual.

As the plant is nurtured, it grows to become beautiful and healthy. This is the result of remembering the nurturing of your growth by the wisdom acquired from other's experiences. As we remember, we become appreciative of what we have learned and that is the interpretation of this proverb:

"The experience of the journey is much more delightful when it is shared and its trials much more bearable than when alone."

Chapter 6: United

"Lift burdens on your own, you'll struggle. Lift burdens with others, you will grow stronger together."

The strength of one can be great, dare one say mighty, but the strength of two united shall become a force to be reckoned with. This is the story of the draft horse. The draft horse is a noble steed of immense strength. A single horse can pull upwards of 8,000 lbs., yet when paired together, can pull 24,000 lbs. This is an astonishing feat of strength in the hooves of two, but when they work in unison, the strength of these beasts increases to a workload of 32,000 lbs., 4 times its's own weight and strength calibrations!

This is what it means to unite. Even when we are on top of the world, the pinnacle of our existence, it is better to work together with a likeminded friend, than to take on all the world alone. The wisdom provided by this force of nature teaches us the importance of teamwork, but ultimately, the importance of unity in the face of adversity.

We see many gifted individuals in life, some we aspire to follow, to become, to carry on their legacy. The beauty of learning from these individuals is that we can grow with them and reach heights they never knew possible. If we could live beyond the life span of the average human, which is calculated to be approximately 79 years old, we could learn so much more and give back to humanity's advancement than our predecessors had originally had time to do. Imagine the lifespan being increased back then? We would have immense vaults of wisdom to change the course of history.

The world is ever evolving, with ideologies, faiths, and beliefs changing throughout the ages. It is up to us to brush past these differences and unite as one to which we can move forward arm in arm, hand in hand, fact and data to accomplish what the previous generations have dreamed to begin. A world where our advancements of society are the fruit of a collaborative effort of people united together, unhampered by the things which we often pit against each other in our everyday lives. The core strength of our civilization does not lie in a superiority complex of individuals or groups but in the fundamental roots of our existence, which we call humanity.

"*Alone, we can make a change in the world, but together, we change the world.*"

Chapter 7: Blinded

"Beware the innocence of delusion."

There are many people in life who will influence you, whether you see it or not. The simplest of influence can be the type of food you eat or the color of which you favor, to the most complex of things such as beliefs and values.

Influence is a natural thing in our lives. It is what we can call a herd mentality, which isn't detrimental in most cases. For example, we have laws in place which we follow, procedures to receive certification, and much more. Society is influenced in one way or another to the extent that influence can be twisted into a dangerous weapon. This is where we must be cautious in how we handle viewpoints that may be regarded as damaging to our wellbeing.

We are often told how we must be in order to be accepted in society. While this is true, there are times where peer pressure becomes so strong, it changes us into something that we are not, or causes us to go with the flow to be “cool”. This passage isn’t about parental authority, or guidance from public officials. This is about forces at work which further agendas, hurt others, and hurt us before we can even realize it. The simplest explanation of this could be drug usage, with some of the most complex like embezzlement.

Influence, like a loaded gun, can be a tool if you used properly, but it can also become a weapon which harms many. The power of influence has changed the course of history many times before and continues to do so today.

It is up to us to exercise caution in how we interpret influences that are beyond our understanding. If you are properly educated on what you are dealing with or discussing with those who are advocating for their viewpoints and beliefs, make your judgement call, consider options, and of course, remember to be well versed in any different views so if a question should arise, you can answer it.

We are all capable of learning from others if we allow ourselves to be, but we are also capable of becoming tainted, manipulated, or destroyed if we blindly trust anyone. Confide with trusted people in your life and do not be afraid to seek their advice. You will save much sorrow.

"The wise seek consul in all things, no matter their experience."

Chapter 8: Trust

"Challenge lies before those who shake hands of alliance with daggers behind their backs."

Trust is a topic of much debate amongst history. Julius Caesar was a prime example of trust being used against him, yet

Oskar Schindler was trusted by Jews during the holocaust to escape the cruel leaders of Nazi Germany.

Trust is one of the hardest things to earn, and one of the easiest to break. It is the glue that holds relationships together, whether they be friendships, marriages, or even business relations. We see trust again and again in our lives. Our ability to trust is affected by many variables in life. Some never trust again, some learn to trust again, and others trust freely, with the ability to discern the good or the bad. There is a difference between being naïve and being experienced.

I have trusted time and time again, to the benefit of forming many relationships in my short time here on earth, and time and time again, that trust has been broken. I have learned to be taken for granted. My kindness is not unconditional, and neither is my love. People have come back trying to win my trust and friendship again, and I have let those people fall to their own peril. I am not responsible for their choices past or present. They are able to go to another, and maybe they have learned from their mistakes, but oftentimes, they justify their mentality and once again fall into the same cycle. I know many individuals like this, who use their victimhood to gain empathy from those who believe them, and once the truth is revealed, they have become a product of their discord.

I do not entertain these people. I simply mind my own business and move on. After all, if the things said about you aren't true, then what have you to gain from engaging fools? We often become bothered with negativity radiating from individuals like this and I find myself pitying them, for their poor outlook on life has clouded their vision of its richness.

In the end, your life is your and yours alone. Despite life being terrible, there is always an ounce of positivity even when all has been lost. The human spirit has proven time and time again to overcome all obstacles.

"The individual who chooses to be what people think they are become the very thing they knew they weren't."

Chapter 9: Integrity

"Sometimes, you can do the good thing or the right thing."

Everyone has their own battles, with just as important of choices as anyone else.

Who are we to judge the importance of a child's game, to the grandeur of a composer of an orchestra? We oftentimes prioritize one over the other which is normal in human nature. As we grow older, our cares for certain things and events changes. Things we were really involved in at a young age are now the times of the past; a memory if even remembered.

Within these choices of life, we often face a battle of our integrity. What is integrity? Integrity is the moral beliefs and values of an individual that plays a key role in our choosing of the journey of life. Some wish to be selfish, some wish to be cruel, to be good, to be evil, to care, to cause chaos. Everyone has a battle in their lifetime, and in those battles, the individual becomes the product of their own intent.

It is common in life that you will meet an individual who cares nothing about integrity and instead wishes to tear down people. Do not worry about them. You will encounter them, and in the long run, karma often takes care of them. Then again, these people sometimes go through life without worry and satisfy their desires but at the end of life, they will go the same route as all humankind has gone: the way of the grave.

Whether you believe in a God, or not, is not my concern. We are certain of one thing, and that is death. When your number is pulled, you cannot escape it. Do not be afraid of death friend, for it is a natural occurrence of life. Take ease in knowing that when you die, your energy will be transferred to the universe amongst the stars.

Some people are afraid of death and these same people are usually the ones who thought they had their lives all together but that is not the case. As I said, karma catches up to every individual whether good or bad, and in the end the toll is paid. Is there injustice? Of course, there is, but that is not our problem, for it rains on the just and the unjust. We are not guaranteed lives of ease or lives at all. It is what it is. Just remember to be the best you can, to walk upright and full of virtue, and hopefully at the end of life, you have made an impact in the world.

“*The potential for greatness is in everyone. Find your passion, refine it, and you will have achieved success.*”

Chapter 10: Perception

"Perception is the difference of value and desire."

What is perception? It is the difference of something from different points of view, like a house or a plot of land. A house is desirable, a plot of land is valuable. One can be lived in, and one can provide a living, but the thing with this is they can be used for the same purpose interchangeably, but it's up to our perception to see the utility in these examples.

Our perception of life can vary. For example, in the previous chapter, we discussed my friend Logan who passed due to cancer. The perception in our views is that he was taken too soon, but if we see he no longer suffers, we are consoled in the fact he is free from the mortal bounds which decreased his quality of life so quickly. Sometimes, our own desires are minimal to the greater picture, as Logan is now among the world after us in which we know not of until we cross the barrier that we call death.

This is seen in everyday life. We sometimes ask ourselves “why me?” or “why them?” but this view is determined by our perception of the situation rather than our understanding of the situation. If we stay up late, we assume we get up late, or if we get up early, our body will be fatigued from lack of rest. If we overhear a rumor, we can assume many things, good or bad, and thus damage relationships or judge the matter without full context. Perception is powerful and many a great thing have been affected by it. Wars have been started over false perception and many heartaches have been born out of it.

Perception has been one of the most powerful attributes that humans possess for the amount of influence it wields. As stated before, influence from perception has the ability to turn the tides for us or against us. We must be careful in making the right judgement calls and pursuing stability when overseeing a matter.

In today's society, we see more and more of perception in our captions, our photos, the like of other photos of interests piquing our interest, and lastly comments to and received about our social media presence. It's amazing how much a simple comment can start many different things throughout the internet. The danger of false perception can lead one downward until they are ultimately destroyed whether emotionally or physically.

We see perception as a valuable tool, and the greatness as well as it's danger in its use. Perception often is useful in making our situations understandable but at the same time detrimental if acted upon wrongly. It is up to us to clear our mind and measure ourselves and the consequences of our actions if we are hasty in judging.

"Perception can change a person. Deception can change the people."

Chapter 11: Worth

"Some of you underestimate yourselves. You all have worth. Find it."

There once was a man who lived down the street from me that passed away. His estate sale featured many items from around the world. I, an avid collector of specific items of value decided to take a look inside the home of this man and see if I could find anything of value. I came across a bell, tarnished with years of oxidation on it which told me one thing: silver!

I immediately scooped it up and later on brought it home with some other things. First, I inspected it, prepped some baking soda mixed with warm water and began to gently remove the tarnish from the bell, which took about 30 minutes. Once it was clean inside out, I held it up to the light to see any places I may have missed but to my amazement and joy, the bell once again shone brightly in the light of my room.

The total cost for this amount of effort and work? About $2.50.

The pawn shop I took it to wanted it for $3. I wasn't planning on selling it, but it was nice to see some value added to it. I took it to a collector of antiques; they offered $25! Lastly, I looked online to see the value of the bell (Wallace and Silversmiths Christmas 2003 Silver Bell) and found some as high as $90! It truly does matter where you take your business, as there is always negotiation for price but the place that knows your worth will often reward you for it highly.

Often in life you will find many people who get to know you, and based off their experience with you, will get an impression of your skills and personality. Unfortunately, sometimes many will get a negative impression of you during a bad time in which you are in. There are many people out there that think of themselves higher than others or think the services we provide are subpar to what they think they should be. It is the reason the world isn't so merciful to those same people when they make a mistake. "What goes around comes around" when it comes to describing karma. The world often dishes out the same treatment in response whether it is that same day or the next year.

Do not let it get to you. There have been many times where I have been treated badly due to a mistake I made, or others have made but used me as the scapegoat. Other times, people are just jerks. It is ok, because in the end, you will find self-worth and hopefully advancement through your reaction the situations that test your spirit. Do not succumb to their level, instead, work to improve yourself and when the time comes, if you should encounter them, let the work of your labor test their attitude. You are valuable, and capable of many skillsets you must discover on your own.

"Forgive but do not forget."

Chapter 12: Intelligence

"I have found that intelligence is not a blessing, but a prerequisite."

Intelligence is something gained by those who wish to learn and throughout the years I have dedicated to study, I have learned a great deal. The intellect of man has brought forth so much good yet much evil alongside it. Mankind itself has never been perfect, nor has it always been humane to every human on the planet. We find with great knowledge of our society comes at levels of understanding. These levels are achieved by learning whether by experience or by study, which in itself is a challenge. The knowledge possessed by those who master it have choice when it comes to using it. Will the outcome be good or evil, or as some would say, "what is evil? What is good?". These individuals open paths into their ideology and philosophy, changing into their current mentality in which they practice their beliefs.

What is it to judge, however? Are we God? Are we higher beings? I say no, but those with truthful knowledge and understanding, are responsible for their decisions to come in life. Some of these are doctors, some are lawyers, political officials, etcetera. There is endless possibility to those who may possesses vast amounts of knowledge and those who squander the opportunity of using or possessing it.

We often see those who influence people, which are within their rights using their talent and experience to show the masses beneficial knowledge with the achieved results. However, a majority of these individuals seem to have a personality of defiance or more plainly "I don't care what other's think, I will do this, or I will do that and prove to them I can." This is absolute stupidity. There is no reason to shout out at those willing to listen that your stance and drive is something to worth noted for. There are countless individuals always doing more than you. You are not special. You are human, with limits and different views on life as any other person on this planet. I said in the last chapter that you are valuable and capable, but you are not a gift to man.

The first difficulty of this generation is that a majority of it seems to think they are the change the world has been waiting and many come to a hard realization that life, itself, does not heed to their whims. If you want changes, you will have to work for it. If you succeed, you will in the end have influenced many, bringing worth to them through you. The second difficulty is simple: humility. Sure, you can post about the dollars you have brought in. You can showcase a new car you may have bought. You can stand in front of a home you bought and want the world to see "Here I have done this. What have you done?" It is simply vain to expect life to revolve around you when in reality, you revolve around life and its nature.

“The principle of confidentiality is the reality of the knowledge you possess and whether it keeps you up at night.”

Chapter 13: The Lying Truth

"If I told you what I knew, you would never believe me, but if I told you what you wanted to hear, you would never doubt me."

Deception is a real thing, and in it, we hide truths that would otherwise, harm our friends, our family, our society, and our world. It does not take much to send it all crashing down, because the risk of telling people what we know could potentially alter the course of our relationships with them, we would rather sell them a lie, a reassurance of hope, something that brings meaning and understanding while placating the individual(s) with a false relief and avoiding all out conflict. We are amazingly good at lying to others because, psychologically, people do not like to live in fear. This is true of many instances as we see such as the media, religion, politics, even in simple scenarios like parenting where a child is reassured of a problem's irrelevance when in reality, the parent is attempting to keep the child calm. We are programmed this way and unfortunately, we live in a day and age where the amount of information, truth, and data, are all overshadowed by the powers that be and any little slip up gets brushed underneath the rug, or ignored, because that's what power is: control. We cannot imagine the amount of darkness that lurks within society, as we cannot imagine things we would do if given the chance. I often ponder the consequences of uncovering truths that we may never know, history that was narrated differently due to interference, lives changed due to 1 or the collaboration of many individuals/governments/organizations that decided to change the world for their benefit. It was never personal; it was only business.

The world is full of lies, some which will never be revealed, and yet, we are promised security, safety, and comfort for accepting it. The status quo of obey, not think has been broken with the rise of the internet, leading some to speculate that in a last effort ditch to keep people blind is to bombard them with ads, clickbait, misinformation, and entertainment in order to confuse them, hoping that a majority will form a hive mindset. The ultimatum is clear, do we accept the lies in exchange for our mundane lives, or do we attempt uncover the truth? We often find ourselves in the midst of knowledge in this age of information, and yet, we can sometimes be biased to the reality of truth and how much it darkens our world view.

As the years have gone on, I have seen more and more lies in order to shut down any opposition. Ideologies that go against some of the laws of logic and morality, and of course, pressure from organizations who wish to profit from those same lies. I have become more cynical mentally, often issuing extreme suggestions in order to curtail this already destructive society, yet I do find myself in my words more stoic, as I always remind myself and my audience that life is what it is, and it is much more than just issuing suggestions to problems at hand, but to rather perform action or to focus on the day-to-day tasks of living.

After all, the choice was always yours, or was it?

"*We often find ourselves lost in darkness, only to discover that we could have opened our eyes the whole time.*"

Chapter 14: Expectations

"Expecting advancement in life is like expecting to catch air with a net."

One thing I've learned is to keep my expectations low. I consider having high hopes risk, even if the odds are given. It is hard to shake the habit of expecting good things when there are variables for bad things to occur alongside them or inconveniences. We address this as bad luck, or karma for actions preceding the current one(s). The notion of expecting nothing yields from many things, including trauma, life choices, and personality. Some suggest we read motivational books or listen to inspirational speeches. Others have used religion of the power of friendship to establish positivity in their mindset, but I say none of these things will actually make a difference when expecting the inevitable. Realistically, I consider myself a sort of stoic, with a hint of positivity. This is different than the positivity and encouragement I give others as compared to when we are alone with our thoughts. This is not negativity, it is realism in a simple, neutral way of seeing life's randomness. To expect the unexpected. To prove the universe's ability to take one instance and escalate it around the environment you are in. Some things are inspired by more than just chance, however.

When presented with the number of variables, one can only place their trust on something they hold in respect to the matter of things. We often see many who take time out of their day to meditate, think, ponder the results of something they are or have hoped for and study the outcome of it. Potential in thinking thoughts of analysis tends to bring a sort of relief to those who wish to search a situation or idea before publishing it. For example, this book you are reading, is it not carefully and meticulously planned out? Was the success left in the hands of those who bought it or in the work of the creators marketing? We see that through hope, we can inspire faith in success but in reality, success comes from preparation and opportunity in which we, the individuals alone must possess at the right times.

Expectations can be high, and in these trying times, we can see that expectations on everyone and everything have multiplied. We see it in movies, political candidates, world events, social media, the stock market, academics, sports, and ourselves. The list goes on and on. One thing can be certain however:

"*If you try to please everyone, you'll only end up being what they want you to be.*"

Chapter 15: Gratitude

"Never forget to be grateful for what you have while you strive for more."

Ungratefulness has prevailed in times before and it certainly is very exposed in the world today. Pick up any phone or tablet (Do we still use those?) and see for yourself the selfishness in people despite their follower status or celebrity status. You'll see it in people's mentality of entitlement to things others have worked for. You see it in race, wealth equality, nations, and economical leverage yet we complain and gripe about our situations. “Well, I’m a victim! where’s my restitution?” “My feelings are hurt!” “My parents said I can’t do this/that!” “They didn’t follow me back!” and of course, the constant dribble of society continues to flood the eyes and ears of those willing to listen or to mock, depending on how you see the situation. I’m for equality, and rights, the wonderful things and movements related to those can be enjoyed today. I’m not talking about those, no, I’m talking about people who’s only source of value comes from them running their mouth or fingers across places like Twitter or Reddit. It's annoying. It's glorified narcissism.

How about improving your situation or starting a movement? There are many nations, the U.S. included that do not know how good they have it. We make a big deal out of little things, because a lot of the big things have either a, been solved, or b, will make the current situation worse. Instead, we turn our focus to things that are trivial, that are easily solved but due to ignorance and emotions, turn into movements of stupidity. On the contrary, organizations and groups in the past few years have been manipulated by the few that have the power and the influence of outside donors adds to the ever-burning dumpster fire of "making a change". I don't condone action, but I do condone mindless drones who regurgitate the words of others without actually knowing what they represent.

Ungratefulness has led us to believe that we have a voice and make a difference to things we see as unfair or injustice when in reality, the truth is that some people just suck and of course, some businesses suck. **PEOPLE SUCK**. Another crazy thing is those same voices and actions are manipulations of higher influences using them to further agendas, line pockets, and funnel resources to escape taxes a lot of the time. You don't have to believe me. You can look up the reasons behind donating to organizations and movements. You can look at the spending, the corruption, and of course, the influence gained from support to use to your advantage. There is a good thing and bad thing about that.

Unfortunately, people will not always agree with me, and I'm not writing to make you agree with me, I'm writing to open the mind of those who refuse to see a bigger picture, a different perception of the matter. Differences in opinion or ideologies, does not equal to intolerance, it only allows for others to share viewpoints not considered in the past. Remember the very thing that matters to those who deem something worth the attention of the masses:

"*Value is reflective of appointment.*"

Chapter 16: Example

"*Make decisions as if there are others following your example.*"

Decisions, decisions. The saying goes that our seemingly limitless options are the very thing that keeps us from providing reasonable examples of doing things on an everyday basis. Our decisions influence the actions and responses of others. In using our influence, we come across a variety of people with different backgrounds and experiences similar to ours or offering newfound revelation compared to ours. We have the opportunity to do a variety of things on a global scale. There's academics, politics, industry, agriculture, healthcare and the list goes on.

Our simplest form of example is providing those younger than us pathways to choose from, to analyze for future reference. Most would not choose a life of crime and evil but there is a percentage that will find themselves in those situations and continue to fuel them unfortunately. Where there is good, there will eventually be some mischief. There are some that will be future figures of history which once again, will be either looked on fondly or with judgement. Blindly following one's example can be detrimental to the advancement of a family, a culture, or even an individual's overall success. The ability to utilize rational thought is a concept that many have given themselves to once they find a reason to question something. However, this in itself can lead to ignorance and stupidity. Yes, stupidity can flow freely form the mouths of those who consider false information the most concrete of facts even when presented with the truth.

We find that in influence, and example, the masses are controlled easily.

Throughout history, many great and many terrible leaders have led the tides of the people and channeled them into a force of great reckoning as well as devout obedience to their causes. The Bolsheviks led by the notorious Vladmir Lenin, The Protestants, led by Martin Luther, the Nazi's led by Adolf Hitler, the United States, led by George Washington. Influence is powerful and when the masses heed to your influence, you can change the world.

The advice in the quote reflects issuing solid examples of integrity, kindness, trust, love, and patience in the current world today. We see so much hate and division for those who have opposing beliefs, customs, and nationalities. The issue in modern society is that the minority have become the majority and, in the process, have become to be aggressive, and unresponsive to having a conversation, lest they themselves are found either ignorant or hypocritical in their doctrines. There isn't a person in this world who truly likes to be wrong or silenced so why do we now? Are we afraid of opposing opinions? Do we lack clear rational reasoning to have a debate? I'm not expressing sympathy for hateful ideologies or racism; I'm expressing concern for the growing number of individuals who think it is acceptable to screech, cancel, and holler at those with values and traditional mindsets that are not the norm, and in doing so fuel the very hate they so preach against. In life, we must strive to come together and find common ground or at least a reasonable compromise because in doing so we can see success because:

"Error breeds resolve."

Chapter 17: Moments and Lifetimes

"The difference between the hustler and the entrepreneur is that one makes money for the moment and the other makes money for a lifetime."

I like money. It helps me do a myriad of things like pay my bills, keep my truck filled up, and allows me to buy my favorite beverage: Redbull. Money is earned through a means of actions pertaining to the performance of duties to receive payment for it. In other words, work. Even if you are a criminal, you have to work at getting the money. Everything involves some sort of effort no matter how miniscule it is. The hustler is a prime example of making money as several small gigs or hobbies can lead one to earning money for the momentary life we live. The entrepreneur, however, is determined to make money for a lifetime and keep the cash flow faucet on for the rest of theirs.

The hustler maintains their lifestyle by performing jobs that provide temporary payouts or extra side money. Their mentality revolves around identifying trends within industries that offer services or products that could net them great gains. The hustler learns to adopt this mentality and attempts to keep the money flowing while all the while changing hats to support their bank account. The risk here being that if there is no stability, risk is the gamble of their entire life and if there is high risk, high reward, stability is thrown out the window. People may argue a hustle is just as good as a long-term business but if it is constantly being changed from painting to photo shoots to swim lessons, you will have to keep the performance high in order to survive. These life commitments are not always the greatest of cash flow as they vary in pay and hoping there are openings available is not exactly wise

The entrepreneur we analyze, focuses on a particular service or product and leverages experience and patience to achieve high gains and expansion. The entrepreneur works hard, often suffering financially before making profit. Sometimes, their efforts fail, and they have to start over once again, suffering from lost time and effort. However, when the entrepreneur does achieve success, their industry of choice nets them gains and they in turn start to build (hopefully) a lasting successful business in which they can eventually profit greatly from, surpassing the hustler in the long run.

The moral of the story is that a hustler, while making gains as fast as they can, is maintaining their position by giving it their all, and if they are not careful, could end up in the same spot when they can no longer. The entrepreneur focuses on something they are proficient in, and while the process is slower, it usually yields much fruit. Sometimes, the hustler becomes the entrepreneur, often stopping to focus on a specific thing that earns themselves an income for life. If we take this concept and apply it to our lives in everything we do, we can become even more rich in value or knowledge as well as financially.

"*One man's business is another's hobby.*"

Chapter 18: Growth

"Growing old is mandatory. Growing up is optional."

The expansion of growth stems from the nurturing of the mind from a young age. The abilities that are born from the proper educational and physical background of an individual are unlimited when looked at from the scope of time itself. The number of prodigies born too early or too late for their time surpasses all human capacity for comprehensive studies as the times before did not allow us to pursue the luxuries we have today. If you were to plant an educated and resourceful individual in let's, say the 1700's, the difference made in advancement and technology would be extravagant given the allowance and acceptance of methods in the modern age, yet one could reason that the only way that could be perceived is by proving time travel is real, and altering the timeline in theory. Technically, creating an alternate timeline parallel to ours is something to be considered.

However, theory aside, there is still an account for maturity. Growing does not only just mean in academics or skill, but it also means that an individual or society has proven to be mature with the matters surrounding those topics with values and morality. An individual who is fully matured will continue to learn and adapt for their age in these subjects even if they do not look it. The growth of an individual is subjective to their understanding of the world and its lessons, life and its teachings, people, and their emotions. It is acceptable to have a period in which you are not mature enough to understand life or people. To be considered an outcast, and an annoyance. I know I once was. I am beyond that now, and often times wonder how my life would have been, had I had just applied myself and matured faster. If I had, perhaps I would have had a better conclusion in my life than now, and possibly better relations with my colleagues of the past. My MBA program was a fresh start and effort to regain a better understanding of people and their lives and to be included as a positive instance rather than an annoyance. At the time of this writing, I still have much work to do, and in the hopes of restructuring my life, I aim to advance further than any of my peers of the past. It is not a competition with others, it is a competition with me.

There are times where I cringe at the way I acted or spoke in the past, because in doing so, I was not taken as serious. We use instances like this to learn and grow, and unfortunately, some never do grow. We age automatically, but mentally, are free to pause growth and stay within a fantasy world we are comfortable in. I have reviewed a lot of my previous posts, stories, videos, and writings with an open mind, and in doing so, have started to change the way I respond in my life. My social circles have grown, my opportunities increased, the amount of advice taken from me common, and respect risen. I do not consider myself entitled to these, as through work we must attempt to maintain and nurture them. It's ok to be young at heart, but it is not ok to be young always. Some people have seen that I have changed, others have not. I am not here to convince them; I am here to convince myself of maturity.

"*We ask for trees, yet we are given seeds. Plant, nurture, grow.*"

Chapter 19: Detachment

"*An individual that has nothing to lose is the one to fear the most.*"

There is no strategy to someone with nothing to lose, only unpredictability. It is a person who has seen loss time and time again, the essence of life, devoid of human emotion. And unpredictable person is a dangerous person if they are against everyone and anyone. You'll see the rendition of the Joker in media and comics; the Joker has the purest form of the "nothing to lose" mindset. There is no agenda to the Joker, only madness. No agenda, only purpose, but what is purpose in the eyes of a madman? What is loss to those who have no care for it? Do we fear the unknown or the unknown person? Is an individual who only sees benefit for themselves and only themselves through meticulous planning to only rise to the top rapidly an inspirational thing or is it an unprecedented danger?

We ask questions like these in times of uncertainty. We look to history to comprehend the purpose behind people who don't have one. Serial killers, warlords, genocidal maniacs, psych patients, all these have been at the forefront of studying the human mind and trying to unlock the secrets of the brain's psychological reasoning. The capacity for knowledge, yet the capacity for chaos is unlimited in the human mind, and yet, researchers still cannot grasp the secrets of it. It is astounding to see the power of it and in the wrong person, can be used intelligently to perform acts of evil. Thus, the same person who has nothing to lose; nothing to hold them back; free from all bonds, responsibilities, and emotions, is one of the most dangerous people to ever come across.

Some say these individuals are narcissists, other's say they're insane, but I say their intelligence comes from detachment. Learning to detach from your entire self is a liberating yet volatile state. We do not encourage chaos or evil. We encourage rationality, lack of emotion, but increased understanding of our fellow man. We work to bring to light inclusion, collaboration, and respect of those willing to build a good society. It is not wrong to be apart from the world, but it is not right to be cold to it. I wrote this quote with the confidence of not worrying about trivial things such as money, clothes, and shelter. I intended to bring a sense of resourcefulness and creativity in order to accelerate our intelligence. A sort of independence and reluctance to just wait for a handout. We as a society have the capacity to survive if we try and if we try in the small things, we can try in the bigger things to build an easier life for our descendants, and this is true. The cycle continues as the world goes through events and unfortunate restructuring such as war and famine.

We are incredibly blessed to be in a day and age where the farthest reaches of research and technology can be accessed within the palm of our hands in a matter of seconds. The access to food in quality and quantity with varieties is a miracle if thought about in comparison to some places in the world. That has been done through the sacrifice of selfless people detached from sole personal gain and instead has chosen to help the world. This is the true definition of detachment.

"I help people not because I expect anything in return, but because of who I am."

Chapter 20: Teammates

"Find a teammate, not a liability."

All people have come to realize they would be better suited to find others of benefit to themselves than to just rely on themselves. I understand the point of view of an introvert, but even the introvert needs assistance at times. Our societal strength is not exactly in numbers, it is within the quality of people we associate with. Learning to operate in a team is not exactly an easy task, as you will have to observe and delegate skillsets, personalities, and workloads within it. This can be as simple as having someone help you with moving boxes or as hard as asking for financial advice from someone more qualified in the subject. Teams are everywhere, not just in work.

You also form teams in relationships whether romantic or platonic. The benefit of teams is added support when you need it. The pooled resource in teams lessens the overall usage of yours or any sole persons. A community operates off of shared resources and industry, often going from trade and barter to currency based as time has shown us. We have gone from trading to commodity-based currency, to fiat currency in the past 150 years of the U.S. Through this and other examples, we achieve the same amount of collaboration as if we were close friends with each resource outlet.

In life, you will find that in all avenues, there will be some sort of teambuilding and collaboration in the outside world whether it be a social club, a store, a church group, academic classes, or even a spouse and family. We all see the structure of teamwork in almost everything we do. Together, we can achieve many great things if we were to sacrifice some of our overall personal gain and share it with others. I am not referring to ideologies, I am referring to people helping other people obtain their goals while fulfilling their own in the long run. It is better to build a foundation and pull others up alongside you than to build the rest of it yourself. Leaving people at the bottom will only make things harder for yourself to build your legacy. If you take time to share ideas and offer support, you will be unstoppable.

My father told me once that the people working together at the end of the day will say “look what we have done” instead of saying “look what I have done”, with the right amount of good leadership. To lead a team or influence others to follow your example as explained a couple chapters ago furthers the value and support of your group if you choose to be a foundational builder. We often see those that build legacies with groups of like-minded people, reaching for goals deemed impossible attempting alone. The benefit of building a team is the soon-to-come fruit of hard labor. Teams established by focusing on oneself tend to fail terribly, due to the selfish nature of bringing people down while ascending but what happens when the step ladder of people ends? You fall a terribly fast way to the ground. We as people, flawed in our ways, tend to forget our past experiences and those who helped us along the way. If we cannot work together, why would we ever think that we could last at the top or even reach it?

"*Wealth lies not in possessions or valuables. It comes from the people you keep close.*"

Chapter 21: Pushing Limits

"There are limits, and there are levels."

Limits and levels are often used to describe the boundaries and goals that we set for ourselves in life. These limits and levels can be physical, mental, emotional, or spiritual, and they can help us to focus our efforts and measure our progress as we work towards achieving our goals. In our previous 2 years following Covid-19, we have seen many people surpass their limits, often having to go to the next level in order to survive.

However, it is important to remember that limits and levels are not fixed or static. They are constantly changing and evolving as we grow and learn new things. It is therefore essential that we continually challenge ourselves and push the boundaries of what we think is possible in order to reach higher levels of achievement and fulfillment. Surpassing a level is not an easy task, nor is a limit. It's like training our bodies in the gym, changing diets, and incorporating exercises to strengthen our bodies.

One way to do this is by setting specific and measurable goals for our wellbeing. This allows us to clearly define what we want to achieve and gives us a roadmap to follow as we work towards our goals. It also helps us to stay motivated and focused, as we can track our progress and see the tangible results of our efforts.

Another way to push the limits and reach higher levels is by learning from our failures and setbacks. Every challenge presents an opportunity for growth and learning, and by embracing these moments and using them as steppingstones to reach higher levels, we can overcome any obstacle and achieve greater success.

Ultimately, the key to reaching new limits and levels is to believe in ourselves and our ability to achieve our goals. By maintaining a positive and motivated mindset, we can overcome any challenge and reach new heights of personal and professional success.

"Going to the next level" can take many forms, such as setting and working towards specific goals, learning new skills and knowledge, or simply striving to be the best version of ourselves. There are many benefits to this in our personal and professional lives. One of the most obvious benefits is the sense of accomplishment and pride that comes from achieving our goals and reaching new levels of success. This can provide a great deal of motivation and satisfaction and can help us to feel more confident and self-assured.

In addition to the personal satisfaction that comes from "going to the next level," there are also numerous practical benefits. For example, by developing new skills and knowledge, we can become more valuable in our social lives. As we push ourselves to be the best we can be, our relationships with others improve greatly building stronger connections and communities, ultimately contributing to the well-being and success of those around us. Our values and actions in the light of aiming for the stars allows us to ignite the flame in others.

"Bright futures await everyone, but sometimes, we forget to take off our sunglasses."

Chapter 22: How Can I?

"The difference between a successful person and a limited person is 'How can I?' and 'How can I?'."

"How can I?" is a phrase that can be used in a variety of contexts and can convey different meanings depending on the context and the tone in which it is used. In one context, "How can I?" might be used to express a sense of determination and a desire to achieve a specific objective or goal. In this sense, the phrase is used as a way of seeking guidance or ideas on how to overcome a challenge or obstacle.

For example, if someone says, "How can I get money?", they might be seeking advice on how to earn more income or save more money. They might be looking for suggestions on how to start a business, invest in stocks, or find ways to reduce their expenses. In this context, the phrase "How can I?" is used as a way of seeking ideas and solutions to a specific problem or challenge.

On the other hand, "How can I?" can also be used in a way that conveys a sense of discouragement or despair. In this context, the phrase might be used to express frustration or a lack of hope in the face of a difficult or seemingly insurmountable challenge. For example, if someone says, "How can I ever get money?", they might be expressing a sense of hopelessness about their financial situation and might feel like they will never be able to achieve the financial security or stability that they desire.

In this context, the phrase "How can I?" is used as a way of expressing a sense of helplessness or despair, rather than a desire to find solutions or ideas. Recognizing the differences in character of the phrase "How can I?", as the way it is used can have a significant impact on our mindset and attitude and can either inspire us to act and work towards our goals or discourage us from even trying, because despite the many benefits of trying to achieve our goals, it is natural to encounter obstacles and setbacks along the way. To avoid discouragement and stay motivated as we strive for greatness, it is helpful to set specific and achievable goals, celebrate small victories, seek support and guidance, and learn from failures and setbacks. Having a plan and set lines of goals, both of which are clear as well as specific can help us to stay focused, motivated, and measure our progress along the way. It is important to make sure that our goals are realistically achievable, as this can help us to avoid becoming discouraged when we encounter challenges. Recognizing and celebrating our progress, no matter how small, can also help us to stay motivated and to build momentum as we work towards our goals.

I have went through this myself, with my businesses, schooling, relationships and even this book, in trying to achieve a goal I had set in mind, knowing that I needed to finish what I started. I have experienced setbacks, loss, and discouragement in writing my book, but I have also found a newfound respect for those who wish to write and those who do not give up in the face of negativity.

"Preparing yourself for downfall is the expectancy of rising up again."

Chapter 23: Wanderers

"Wanderers are not always lost; they show up at the right time for their appointed purpose."

The wanderer is an individual who roams or travels without a specific destination in mind. They may seem lost to those around them, but they are often on a journey of self-discovery and personal growth. These wanderers may not know exactly where they are going, but they trust that they will arrive at the right place and the right time. They believe that everything happens for a reason and that their path will lead them to their appointed purpose. Wanderers are not afraid to take risks and step outside of their comfort zone. They embrace the unknown and see it as an opportunity to learn and grow. Their main strength lies in the volatility of life's offerings and how they can use them to further themselves. In other words, expecting the unexpected.

Despite their uncertainty of how life will treat them, wanderers are not lost. They are simply following their own path and trusting that it will lead them to where they need to be. Wanderers may wander for a variety of reasons, including a desire for adventure, a search for meaning, or a need for personal growth. Whatever their motivations, they are driven by a sense of purpose and a belief in their own abilities. Wanderers may face challenges and setbacks along their journey, but they are resilient and refuse to give up. They know that every experience, good or bad, is a valuable learning opportunity. They know who they are and what they want, and they are willing to take the necessary steps to get there.

Wanderers, who may seem solitary, are far from alone on their journey. They meet other like-minded individuals along the way and form meaningful connections with them. These connections can provide support, guidance, and encouragement during difficult times. Wanderers are not "lost" in the way society has framed them because they have the courage to follow their hearts and pursue their dreams. They are not afraid to take the road less traveled and create their own path in life. They also tend to forge a deep understanding of themselves and their surroundings throughout their maturity along the path they have set on. They are attuned to the world around them and are able to navigate through life with confidence and grace as their wisdom guides their actions more and more. A strong sense of purpose and meaning in their lives, is driven by their passions and goals, and they know that their journey is leading them towards something greater. I understand the wanderer can be compared to many of us trying to find our life's purpose. I see the similarities between those who think they know their purpose to questioning it. We strive to adapt and compromise but are we really following our dreams or are we settling for dreams set before us by others?

In the end, wanderers are not lost because they show up at the right time for their appointed purpose. They may not know exactly what that purpose is, but they trust that it will be revealed to them in due time. They embrace the unknown and are open to whatever the journey has in store for them.

"I'd rather be remembered for how I impacted people's lives rather than how society viewed me."

Chapter 24: Life

"Let us not forget the blessing of life."

This is the last chapter. If you have made it to this page, I commend you and wish to thank you for reading this portion of the book. When I started doing all my little quotes and sayings in 2020, the world was in a dark place and even though some of it has lightened up since them, it is still dim in comparison to pre-2020. I will now express my final saying for this first volume of the "Go Dark" series: Life's blessing.

Life is a precious and miraculous gift, and it is up to each of us to make the most of it. Living life to the fullest means embracing every moment and seizing every opportunity that comes our way. It means taking risks, trying new things, and pushing ourselves to be our best selves. When we live life to the fullest, we open ourselves up to a world of possibilities and experiences that can enrich and transform us.

One of the greatest blessings of life is the opportunity to connect with others and form deep, meaningful relationships. The chance to pursue our passions and follow our dreams is unlimited regardless of our physical and mental limitations. When we prioritize our health and well-being, we are better equipped to handle whatever life throws our way. If we are true to ourselves and our passions, we can experience a sense of purpose and fulfillment that is truly extraordinary. Life is full of challenges and setbacks, but it is also full of immense amounts of joy, wonder, and beauty. When we are open to these experiences and embrace them, we can find true happiness and contentment. The opportunity to learn and grow, whether through formal education, new experiences, or personal reflection, we have the power to continually develop and improve ourselves.

Life is also full of opportunities to give back and make a positive impact on the world around us. Whether it's through volunteer work, charitable giving, or simply being kind to others, we can all make a difference in the lives of those around us. The blessing of life is that it is always changing and evolving. Each day brings new challenges and opportunities, and it is up to us to make the most of them. When we live life to the fullest, we can discover parts of ourselves that we never knew existed. We can tap into our creativity, find new talents, and develop new skills.

It is also full of surprises and unexpected twists and turns. These moments can be scary, but they can also be incredibly exciting and rewarding. When we embrace the unknown and stay open to whatever life has in store for us, we can experience true adventure and growth. Life is short, and it is up to us to make the most of every moment. We have the power to make our lives into whatever we want them to be, and when we embrace that power, the wonders of life are truly limitless.

> "*We often blind ourselves to the beauty of life because we focus on things that do not necessarily concern us, thus casting a shadow over the beauty of the moment rather than the unpromised tomorrow.*"

Thank you for reading.

May your travels be numerous, safe, and your memories bright.

-Alexander Bejar

www.ingramcontent.com/pod-product-compliance
Lightning Source LLC
La Vergne TN
LVHW012100160826
845678LV00014B/2887

9798370276804